687

391

before the last

Dress and Fashion

Dress and Fashion

Olive Ordish

Line drawings by Gwen Mandley

London

Routledge & Kegan Paul

First published in 1974
by Routledge & Kegan Paul Ltd
Broadway House, 68–74 Carter Lane,
London EC4V 5EL
Filmset and printed in Great Britain by
BAS Printers Limited, Wallop, Hampshire
ISBN 0 7100 7790 4

Frontispiece: *A fashion portrait from* Vogue.

Contents

'. . . all the business of life is to endeavour to find out what you don't know by what you do'

John Whiting *Marching Song*

Editor's preface

There is hardly anybody who is not interested in clothes. Whether we are rich or poor, young or old, tall, short, fat or thin, most of us realise that it is worth while choosing what we wear so as to make the best of ourselves.

Never, until our time, have ordinary families been able to dress fashionably. Even fifty years ago the differences in living standards between rich people and all the rest were enormous. Nowadays these differences are getting smaller and smaller, fashion is changing faster than ever before, and clothes are made in very different ways and of new materials.

There is a saying that 'fine feathers don't make fine birds' and, certainly, nobody is a kinder person, or braver, more honest or more interesting *because* they have nice clothes. But if we wear clothes that suit us, then we are likely to feel better and to be more confident and more relaxed.

Most of us take our clothes for granted once we have bought them and do not think very much about what they are made of, where they came from, or who has made them. This book tells you something about these things and was written to help you to look carefully at clothes and to think about what you find. It shows you what you may never have noticed before and — more important — it can help you to find out for yourself.

If you are planning to do a project about fashion you will have to use your eyes and your imagination. You will need to talk to all sorts of different people and to collect pictures and samples from all kinds of places. You will, of course, want to arrange the information and ideas and pictures you have collected in the best order. You may have your own ideas about arrangement, but the headings and chapters in this book will serve as a guide. When you have read it you may find that your eyes and your judgment are sharpened and that buying clothes has become far more interesting than it was.

M.H.

Thinking about clothes

The materials of our clothes

Influences on what people wear

Ideas about your project

Most of us take our clothes very much for granted. Looking in a shop window we may see a garment we need or think would suit us. If we have enough money we buy it.

Where did it all come from?

But how did it reach that shop window? Who designed and made it? What sort of material is it made of and where did that come from?

Let us suppose a girl is wearing a woollen pullover, a silk scarf, cotton jeans, nylon tights and leather sandals.

(a) Very likely the raw material of her jersey once roamed the Australian hills on the back of a sheep.

(b) The silk began as a cocoon wrapped round a chrysalis in Italy.

(c) The cotton in her jeans came from the fluffy seed pod of a shrub growing, maybe, in the southern states of the USA, while

(d) the secret of producing nylon thread from petroleum to make her tights was discovered by chemists in a laboratory.

(e) Her sandal leather – perhaps *you* would like to find out what it once was and what countries it could have come from?

(f) If she is the lucky possessor of a real gold ring or brooch, remember that the gold was dug up from deep under the ground, most likely by a toiling African miner.

The girl's brother might be wearing a pullover knitted by his aunt from wool she bought while on holiday in Scotland. His cotton corduroy trousers are made of blended cotton, some of which came from Egypt and some from the West Indies. He bought his socks very cheaply because they were manufactured in Hong Kong, where people work for very little money. The cotton they were made from, however, was first imported from India.

All these raw materials had to be processed, transported and manufactured into their final shape. Someone must have sat in front of a drawing board thinking out the shape of your dress or the design on your scarf, planning the colours, making a sketch and hoping that it would be accepted. Expert workers have been busy cutting and making up patterns. Buyers and agents have worked hard to get the goods into the shop.

All this and more has gone into the making of your everyday costume.

Changes of fashion

As you know, fashions have changed continually through the ages. It is amusing to track down the very different ideas of what was fashionable from century to century. Sometimes it was considered smart for ladies to pile their hair high, pinch in their waists and wear huge round skirts. At other times their

Could you make a map like this, showing where the material in your own clothes probably came from?

heads had to look small and neat and their figures to appear slender all the way down.

Men's fashions changed just as much. In one period their clothes would be stiff and starchy, in another loose and flowing. Sometimes clothes tended to be richly decorated, at others plain and simple.

How do these changes arise? Do they just come from a desire to look attractive or different? Or are they partly caused by outside events and ideas? Think about it and see if you can decide.

Certainly clothes are not worn only to be warm and decent. How many other motives can you think of?

Fashion has so many connections

Dress and fashion are connected with history, geography, art and science. They are bound up, too, with economics and psychology, that is to say with money matters and human nature. Imagine that in Country A there are few very poor or very rich people, and nearly everyone has to work for a living. In Country B, on the other hand, there is a rich, idle class of people while most of the other inhabitants are poverty-stricken peasants. Do you suppose fashions would be the same in both countries? If not, in what way would they be likely to differ? And so you see that the subject of dress is much wider than you might think at first and, if you plan to do a project on some aspect of clothing, there is a wealth of subject matter to choose from.

Possible projects

a) You could make a study of one kind of fabric, tracing its history and its production from the raw state to the finished article. Silk, for example, is made into various materials, such as taffeta, chiffon and satin, by treating it in different ways. You might collect cuttings of as many fabrics derived from silk as could be found.

Maps, photographs, pictures and picture postcards of its lands of origin could be included as well as illustrations of its various stages and of ancient and modern machinery used for its manufacture. By observation and talking to people in the trade you could find out its chief uses and its good and bad qualities. Pictures of historical costumes and modern dresses made in this fabric could also be used as illustrations.

(b) One of the careers stemming from the clothing trade would make a promising subject. Take design, for example. There is the artistic side concerned with drawing and shape, colour and texture, but there are also practical considerations such as cost, choice of fabric and suitability to a particular kind of customer.

Sketches, brochures, photographs, colour schemes, patterns cuttings and calculations of cost would all have their place in that project.

(c) The fashion trade has many branches — children's clothes shoes, sportswear, and so on. You might make a special study of one of those. Under the heading of Salesmanship and Display, for instance, you could include different kinds of clothes shops and the jobs connected with them, as well as window display, advertising and fashion modelling.

(d) An interesting project could be made on the fashions of some past century, and how they developed in the course of that hundred years. Not only the general shape could be dealt with but also the materials and dyes that could be obtained at the time and what style of hairdressing, shoes and patterns were popular then. Remember that different sorts of people tended to dress differently. Children, farm workers, courtiers, scholars and townsmen each had a style of their own within the general fashion.

(e) Boys and girls interested in engineering or chemistry could look into spinning, weaving, dyeing and the invention of synthetic fabrics.

But whatever subject you choose, make sure your finished project is good to look at. The writings, newspaper cuttings, diagrams, illustrations and objects should be arranged in a sensible order and yet be so varied that it is a pleasure to turn the pages and see what comes next.

Questions and suggestions for things to do are scattered about this book because it is much more interesting to discover some things for yourself than to have everything told to you.

Processes

How early man made garments

Spinning and weaving

The change to making fabrics in factories

Dyeing fabrics and printing patterns on them

What is fashionable depends a good deal on the kind of materials available, the width of cloth woven, and how much people at the time know about cutting, sewing and dyeing.
The first garments were probably pieces of skin and fur joined together with thongs passed through holes or slits. The hides had to be carefully scraped and dried or they would have decayed and smelt terrible. In some tribes, such as the Eskimos, the women chewed the leather to make it soft.

Spinning
It must have happened over and over again that someone — probably a woman — plucked hairs out of the fluffy fleece of a wild goat or sheep and twisted them between her fingers. She may have planned to use the twist as a thong, or perhaps she was just doodling. She soon found that a thread began to form. If she kept adding new strands overlapping with the others, and twisted them tightly enough, quite a long, strong yarn could be produced. It seemed a good idea to wind it on to a stick with a knob fixed to the lower end. As the stick (now known as a spindle) hung down on the thread it could be given a twirl now and again and so would continue to revolve of its own accord, which all helped the twisting process. That was the earliest spinning machine.
You can try this primitive form of spinning yourself. Get some fibre such as sheep's wool (from a crafts shop, or picked from hedges), combings, terylene fibre (from a boat chandler), or even cotton wool, though this last is not very good. Fix the

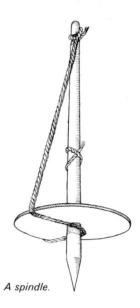

A spindle.

fibre to a forked stick held in your left hand. (Can you find the name given to this forked stick?) It helps if you first card the fibres, that is comb or straighten them so that they lie side by side. With your right hand pluck out the hairs and twist them. As soon as you have a long enough thread you fasten it to the spindle by knotting it under a notch. Go on twisting and every now and again give the spindle a twirl. As your thread grows longer twist more of it round the spindle.

Weaving

It is very likely that men learnt to weave even before they could spin. They wove mats and baskets out of rushes and canes. So as soon as they had learnt to make good thread it must have occurred to them to weave it into fabric for clothes.

The simplest form of weaving is like darning. But you must fasten the lengthwise threads to something solid first.

Any device for weaving is called a loom. To make a very simple loom use a fixed bar such as a towel rail and tie a good many equal lengths of coarse wool or string side by side all along it. Fasten the other ends to another bar, movable this time, or even to your belt. These lengthwise threads are called the warp.

Now tie one end of a whole spool of the same thread to a little notched stick, the shuttle, used like the needle in darning. Pass this over and under alternate threads of the warp, then back again and so on, pushing each new line up against the one before. The crosswire thread is known as the woof or weft.

Spinning and weaving develop

Spinning was considered woman's work. It was often done by the unmarried women — hence the word 'spinster' — and for thousands of years they twirled their spindles by hand, gradually learning how to make finer, stronger yarn. Then the spinning wheel was invented to turn the spindle for them.

When mechanical looms were invented in the eighteenth century, however, there was such a big demand for yarn that not even the best spinning wheels could produce it quickly enough. So in 1764 James Hargreaves invented a means by which several spindles could be turned at once by a single person, and other mechanical improvements soon followed.

The art of weaving did not stand still either. In 1620 a Dutchman invented a loom that could weave six ribbons at a time. The ribbon-makers were so afraid of losing their jobs that they rioted and laws were passed against using the machines. Trouble of that sort often arises even today when new machines are

Weaving cloth in Guatemala, Central America.

introduced. See if you can find out about any recent strikes caused by men's fears for their jobs.

In the eighteenth century mechanical improvements came thick and fast. One of the first was John Kay's flying shuttle patented in 1733, which worked twice as fast as the old method. By 1785 there were power-driven looms. Can you find out who invented them?

The industrial revolution

It was new English inventions of this kind that started off the great change in our lives now known as the industrial revolution. See if you can find out about any other machines invented at that time.

The spinning machines and mechanical looms became too big to be used in the workers' cottages as before and the work had to be done in factories. Today we have huge, noisy textile mills working at high speed and producing vast quantities of fabric, wide, narrow, flat or tubular. There are all sorts of new textiles, weaving patterns and mixtures. In some of the newest looms the weft is shot through the warp not by a shuttle but by a jet of water or air.

Visits to textile mills can often be arranged for people who are interested in modern cloth manufacture and there are still a few hand-weavers who work at home and make beautiful materials.

Dyes and ancient colorants

Brightly coloured clothes are exciting to wear. The oldest known colorants were ochre made from a special reddish or yellow earth, and carbon made from burnt wood. Both were used by the ancient cavemen for painting wall pictures, and probably for clothes and body painting as well.

Thousands of years ago there was already a wide range of colours produced from natural sources. Blue dye was obtained from woad and indigo plants, red from the madder plant, yellow from saffron. The robes of the ancient Roman emperors were dyed with purple from a special sort of shellfish which was found near the city of Tyre in such quantities that the colour became known as 'Tyrian' purple.

There are animal, vegetable and mineral dyes. Try to find out what dyes came from (a) insects, (b) tree bark and (c) iron salts. It would be interesting to collect plants and earths that can be used to make dyes.

New colours

The discovery of America in 1492 added a new colour to our rainbow of dyes, a very bright red from the tiny cochineal insect which was found in the New World. This dye later became the colour basis of the British soldier's scarlet uniform.

A British officer of the Royal Marines in dress uniform. His tunic is scarlet (1832).

B

In the early nineteenth century, however, scientists became interested in producing dyes from chemical mixtures. These synthetic dyes were cheaper and easier to obtain and the colours were often more brilliant than those from natural sources, though not so soft and subtle.

In 1856 two new colorants were invented by chemists and given the names mauve and magenta. Before long nearly all the old natural dyes had been replaced by synthetic ones.

The process
Material has to be treated with a chemical known as a 'mordant' before it will absorb the colour properly.

The basic equipment for dyeing is a dye bath or tub, a colorant and some water to dissolve it in. The fabric is then moved about in the liquid until it is evenly coloured. Sometimes the colour is 'fixed' by boiling or by chemical means. Try dyeing a piece of material yourself.

Fabric printing
But what if you want a pattern on your fabric?

The most primitive way is to paint it on, but that takes a very long time. Several quicker ways have been invented, some not very different from the printing of books.

Block printing
I expect you have made potato and lino cuts and know that you can either cut away the parts you do not want to print, or cut the design into the surface and fill the cut parts with colour, wiping it off the rest.

Wet colour used on fabric runs too easily, so the dye must be made into a paste with starch, gum or some other thickener. A different block is needed for each colour. When the pattern is to be repeated all over the cloth the arrangement and the points at which the designs meet have to be carefully worked out.

Early printing was done in more or less the same way and you could experiment with cloth-printing yourself.

Roller printing

In about 1740 cloth-printing was made easier by cutting the pattern on to rollers like those of an old-fashioned mangle, and passing the fabric between them. This is the system most often used today. It is used for printing newspapers too.

Batik printing

This is done by covering the part you *don't* want to dye, with wax or some other waterproof substance. Can you think why it could be said that the 'mordanting' mentioned on page 10 is the opposite to 'batik'?

Silk screen printing

A method which is growing popular is silk screen printing, which works like a stencil. The silk is stretched on a frame and the design drawn or photographed on to it. Then the non-print area is blocked off with lacquer and the colour painted or sprayed through the rest of the screen. Again a different screen must be used for each colour. Today it can all be done by machine.

3   Materials

Four natural fibres

Man-made fibres: rayon, nylon and others

There are four main types of natural fibre used for making clothing textiles: wool, cotton, silk, linen.

Wool

Wool, as you know, is shorn from the coats of sheep or other fleecy animals such as camels and goats. It is by far the most important animal fibre.

Sheep can be specially bred or cross-bred to produce better fleeces. The wool strands of some British types grow an average of 25·4 cm (10 in.) a year. The famous Spanish merino sheep grow only 6·35 cm (2·5 in.) of wool in that time, but it is so dense that there may be as many as 50,000 fibres to 6·45 cm^2 (1 sq. in.). Poor food, drought and disease all have a harmful effect on the quality of the fleece.

'There's nothing like wool', as people used to say, for warmth, crease resistance and bouncing back into shape.

The story of wool

Wool was known in very ancient times. In the Middle Ages the wool industry supplied our richest trade, and many of the beautiful old churches in wool-growing districts were paid for by wealthy wool merchants. English and Scottish wool and woollen goods still have the highest reputation abroad.

In the nineteenth century English sheep were exported to Australia, North America and New Zealand. In 1960 Australia exported 840 million kg (1,680 million lb.) of wool.

Worsted is made from a special type of wool fibre and is spun by a different method. If you get the chance, compare worsted with ordinary wool in a shop, feel both kinds carefully and think of words to describe the differences. Anyone dealing with wool in a project should write to the International Wool Secretariat, 6 Carlton Gardens, London SW1, for information.

Cotton

Cotton is the most widely used textile fabric in the world. It is made from the fluffy fibres attached to the seeds of the cotton plant and was first cultivated in southern Asia over 3,000 years ago.

The Arabs and later the Crusaders brought it to Europe. The fabric was first heard of in England in the thirteenth century, but did not come into general use here until nearly 500 years later.

About 200 years ago the cotton plant was introduced into the southern part of what is now the USA, which soon became one of the great cotton-growing areas of the world.

Cotton is strong and washes beautifully but is not as soft and warm as wool. It is made into a wide variety of cloths such as

A cotton plant.

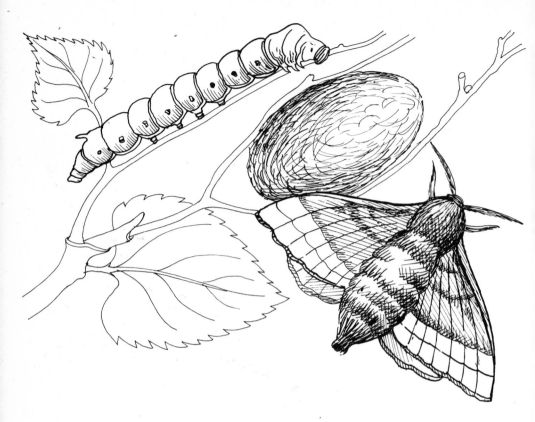

The stages of a silkworm: *caterpillar, cocoon and moth.*

cotton sheeting, corduroy and muslin. Can you find the names of three others?

Silks

A silkworm is not a worm, in fact, but a caterpillar, usually that of the *Bombyx mori* moth. Can you find out what unusual kind of tree the *Bombyx mori* lives and feeds on?

When the time comes for it to become a pupa, the sleeping mid-way stage between caterpillar and moth, it begins to spin a thread from its mouth. For two days and nights it spins without stopping until it has wrapped itself in two miles of continuous filament so fine that fourteen fibres of it must be twisted together to make one usable thread.

Silk drapes beautifully and is lustrous and fine. Although there are some remarkable synthetic imitations they have not quite the feel and quality of the real thing.

It is woven into a number of different fabrics — satin, chiffon, velvet . . . How many more can you discover? Velvet has what is called a 'pile' — so have most carpets. How is a pile woven into a textile?

Linen
The fourth natural textile is linen. You could do some detective work yourself on this material. Find out what and where it comes from and any other interesting facts about it, comparing it with cotton, wool and other materials.
Can you name one or two natural materials, not textiles, used for clothing?

Man-made fibres
At the end of the last century scientists became interested in the idea of manufacturing textile fibres from quite different materials by means of chemicals, and success came in 1892. But do not forget that even 'chemicals' have to come from some natural substance in the first place.

The viscose method
Wood and cotton waste, which are largely made of a material called cellulose, can be reduced to a pulp. Two English research workers experimented with this pulp. They soaked it, dried it, broke it up, dissolved it again and added various chemicals during the process. Finally they forced the mixture through a nozzle pierced with tiny holes, which they called a spinneret, after the spider's web-making organ. Out came fine silky filaments that could be woven into cloth. Dye could be added to the mixture before it was turned into thread.
This way of producing artificial fibres was called the viscose method and the textile thus obtained was given the name of 'rayon'. The various textile manufacturers who make this kind of material give their products special trade names such as 'Celanese', but they all come under the heading of 'rayon'.
Look among your own clothes or among the fabrics displayed

in a shop and see how many labels you can find bearing the words 'viscose rayon' with an additional trade name.

Polyamides and other synthetic fibres

The scientists continued their research and new ways of making synthetic fibres were invented.

As you may know, matter is made up of minute particles known as molecules. The chemists actually managed to change the arrangement and size of some of these molecules.

Materials such as petroleum, coal and agricultural waste were soaked, and then treated with immense heat under pressure. Chemicals were added, they were heated again, until their simple molecules were transformed into giant, chain-like molecules called polymers. The 'polymerised' material, could then be made into the textile fibre we know as *nylon*. A variant of polymer fibre is called *polyester*.

Nowadays two types of textile, either natural or man-made, are often combined to form a new fabric possessing the good qualities of both.

Now continue your investigation of textile labels and see how many names of synthetic or partly synthetic textiles you can collect. The kinds described above are the most usual, but there are others. Clothing fabrics can even be made from glass.

A measure of fineness

When a girl is dressing for a party she probably wears 12-denier tights while her grandmother chooses 60-denier stockings for hard wear. What does 'denier' mean?

The standard length of a skein of silk is 450 m. If such a skein weighed only 1 denier ($= \frac{1}{20}$ or ·05 of a gramme – a tiny weight), it would be incredibly fine. To weigh 10 deniers ($= \frac{1}{2}$ or 0·5 of a gramme) the same length of thread would have to be ten times thicker. And so the thickness of the fibre making up tights is measured in deniers.

Desirable qualities

Few of us have much spare time and most of us have to travel quite often by bus, car or train, so it is very important that the fabric used for our clothes should be easy to care for and non-crushable. In some clothes one can look very smart until one sits down for the first time and gets up again all creased and crumpled! Labels often tell us how a garment should be washed and ironed, or if it should be dry-cleaned. Remember to look! What do *you* consider the most desirable qualities in a dress fabric or material for trousers apart from its appearance? Copy down this list of qualities and mark them 1, 2, 3, etc. to show what, in your view, is their order of importance:

Washable, Non-iron, Non-crease, Fadeless, Long-wearing. You can probably think of other qualities to add to your list.

4   The why and wherefore of clothes and fashion

National costumes and peasant costumes

The purpose of clothes

The leaders of fashion and the followers

The influences upon what we wear

Throughout Europe and America and many other parts of the world the style of dressing is more or less alike at any one time, but it changes as the years go by. Although in the early days of western civilisation the change was very slow it grew gradually faster until today we think some of last year's fashions quite out of date.

In Asia and Africa, on the other hand, except where they have taken to European dress, clothes vary very much from place to place and from country to country, but fashion hardly develops from one century to the next. The national costumes of India, Japan and Egypt are very like they were a hundred years ago.

Peasant costume

Of course there are some very attractive national costumes in Europe too, but they are mostly so-called peasant costumes and not for everyday wear. When times were prosperous the country people would adapt the fashion of the day to their own liking to wear for best. Then, perhaps because farm prices went down and they could not afford new clothes for a long time, that way of dressing became fixed and turned into a tradition. Most of the surviving styles of peasant costume date from between 1600 and 1800.

You may have seen peasant costumes worn by national folk dance companies on television or at festivals and on dolls sold to tourists. In many parts of Britain, picturesque national dress is worn by Indians and Africans living here.

A lovely appliqué picture can be made by tracing figures in peasant or national costume and sticking on small pieces of material, ribbon or tinsel.

Why do we wear clothes?

Well, that seems obvious at first, doesn't it? For warmth, modesty and to look attractive, of course. But the deeper we go into it, the less simple the question becomes and the more often we find ourselves answering, 'Yes, but . . . .'

Traditional Austrian peasant costumes.

Warmth? Yes, but by no means all the clothes we wear help to keep us warm, and girls wearing mini-skirts and nylon tights will face the iciest winds.

Modesty? Yes, but different times and places have such different ideas of what is decent. In Europe until after the First World War it was considered immodest for women to show that they had legs, but they might expose their faces as much as they liked. In the Middle East, however, modest women used to veil their faces but wear trousers, and many of them still do both. A girl in a bikini does not shock us nowadays, but great-great-aunt Agatha would have been speechless with horror.

Attractive clothes

There is no doubt that a very important reason for our choice of clothes is to make ourselves attractive. Yes, but whom do we seek to please? Girls like to attract boys, of course, and boys have no objection to being admired by girls. But we want our workmates, classmates and friends of our own age and sex to approve of us too. Perhaps when we are in doubting mood we even want to assure *ourselves* that we are the sort of characters we would like to be — sophisticated type, crazy Bohemian, tough guy, nature girl, frivolous or serious, as the case may be. Take a boy who likes to speed on a motor-bike with his friends. He buys himself a nail-studded leather jacket with a death's head on the back and a dashing pair of boots. Do you think he chooses those clothes (a) to attract girls, (b) to be one of the crowd, or (c) to feel himself a tough, devil-may-care sort of fellow?

You might have a debate with two friends about it on the lines one sometimes sees on television.

Uniforms

Uniforms are special clothes that distinguish one particular group of people from the population as a whole — whether the group be soldiers, nurses, hippies or skinheads. Can you think of other kinds of uniform-wearer?

In the old days warriors' uniforms were often designed to alarm the enemy. Feather head-dresses and bearskin hats made them look taller than ordinary human beings. The silver braiding on the uniform of the Death's Head Hussar before the First World War outlined his ribs and leg-bones as if he were a skeleton.

How do fashions arise and change?

None of these reasons explains why fashions change. Once having got a useful and attractive collection of garments, why don't people go on wearing the same sort of clothes? Can it be explained?

One reason, surely, is just that we humans like change. After a long time we get tired of the same style and a fresh shape or colour seems refreshing and exciting. But not just any new look will do. It has to be one we are ready for, a fashion in tune with the times. A new and different outfit makes us feel a new and different person.

Who are the fashion leaders?

Who starts new fashions anyway? Who do you think has most influence on what we wear?

(a) the top dress designers
(b) royalty
(c) the very rich
(d) film and television stars
(e) natural leaders
(f) the general public

Put these in what you consider to be their order of importance. Your list would have been very different a hundred years ago.

Keeping up with the Joneses

There is another explanation of changing fashions quite apart from mere love of the new, and that is the desire to show off wealth or importance (our standing or 'status', as they say). Most of us want to dress more or less like our friends and neighbours — but some people like to dress just a little better. All through history the people at the top — the rulers, the court, the rich and important — have tried to dress in a way that marked them off from others. Some fashions were designed to make it plain that the wearer never had to do any hard physical work — very high head-dresses, for example, or sleeves that dangled to the floor, or the long, long finger-nails of the mandarins and the poor little crushed feet of the ladies in ancient China.

There is a story told of Madame Dubarry, the mistress of Louis XV, King of France. She complained to her shoemaker that her new shoes had hardly lasted any time at all. 'But, Madame' he replied with a shocked expression, 'Madame must have *walked* in them!'

When the ordinary people were all very poor it was quite easy for the fortunate few to look different. In prosperous times, however, some of those people became better off and began to climb the ladder. Before long their clothes were looking very like those worn in high society. 'That will never do', thought the people at the top, and promptly changed their style of dressing. But those annoying climbers kept catching them up, and so they had to keep on inventing new fashions to keep one step ahead. Occasionally the rulers went so far as to pass laws forbidding anyone below a certain level from wearing, say, gold braid or ermine fur, but these so-called 'sumptuary laws' were continually broken.

Do you think this 'keeping up with the Joneses' still happens today in a different way? Have you noticed any feeling of that sort at school? Is it a good idea to have school uniforms to keep down rivalry in clothes? What are the objections to school uniform?

But why like that?

So fashions change. But why do they change in one way rather than another? Why do skirts become long and wide in one period and short and narrow in another? There are as many theories as there are experts.

It's all because of politics, they say — or economics or sex or art and literature or new discoveries and scientific inventions.

Certainly war, revolution and hard times, like their opposites, do make a difference to the way we dress. Sometimes a political opinion is shown by wearing a special article of clothing. For instance, do you know what a scarlet tie indicated in 1920 or what a black shirt meant in Italy in 1930? It is also true that scientific inventions and the discovery of new countries bring new materials and fresh ideas.

A mixture of all these influences, what we might call 'the spirit of the age', affects fashion as much as it does everything else — ideas, architecture, art, books, amusements and manners. One writer thinks that the clothes and the buildings of a period resemble one another. For example, that the long pointed sleeves, hoods and head-dresses worn in 1400 look like the 'gothic' arches of the same date, and the tall early Victorian top-hats are the same shape as the tall factory chimneys that sprang up in all the manufacturing towns at that time. If late medieval clothes go with pointed arches, what sort of arch do you think would go with Henry VIII? And can you see any relationships between modern building or furniture and the clothes we wear?

What sort of arch at the time of Henry VIII?

1430.

Henry VIII, 1536.

Shelley, the poet, in about 1815.

The latest ideas, books, plays, rock singers and so on naturally affect the ideals of young people. These, in turn, affect the sort of clothes they wear. The influence of the Beatles a few years ago is an example. Do people try to look like the top pop stars today? Look at this picture of the poet Shelley in about 1815. His generation had abandoned the stiff, artificial costume and wigs of their fathers. His hair and open collar tell us plainly that he had romantic ideas about life and was a lover of freedom.

Do you think modern ideas have had any effect on present fashions?

Sixty years ago the needy clerk would ink the shiny patches on his worn suit and the poor governess would mend her glove so that the darn did not show. They were too proud to let people know how little money they had. Now young people pay extra to have their new jeans patched and faded for them. Is one pretence any more phoney than the other?

Fashions never stop changing. In 1990, when your children look at pictures of today's young people they will see at once that their clothes date from the 1970s, and you will hear that eternal cry of 'How funny you looked then, Mum (or Dad)!'

C

5 English costume through the ages

How do we know?

Hearing about new fashions

Changing styles from 1600 to today

How do we know what our ancestors wore?

Trying to find out how people dressed more than 500 years ago is like looking at a crowded market place through a pinhole. We can only glimpse a few of the passers-by and cannot always be sure of the details. There must be a great many figures — and fashions — that we never see at all.

So much of the evidence has been destroyed. The clothes themselves have rotted away, the wall-paintings have faded, the tapestries fallen to pieces. Evidence still remains, however, in those exquisite illuminated manuscripts, and on tombs, church brasses, windows and other objects depicting men and women as they looked at the time.

As the years went by, more pictures were painted, printing was invented, more tapestries and statues survived. Even some of the actual clothes are to be found in museums. The nearer we get to the present day the richer the evidence becomes.

On the trail

Once having got a good general idea of the subject it is much more interesting to do some research of your own than to rely entirely on pictures of what other people have seen.

There are fine collections of costumes in various museums up and down the country, e.g. the Victoria and Albert Museum in London and the Assembly Rooms at Bath. See if there are some in your local museum.

These garments will show you the actual materials and colours used at the time, and how the cloth was cut and trimmed.

But, alas, some of the life seems to go out of ancient dresses, however carefully preserved. You will have to imagine the faded party gown as it looked, all crisp and fresh, when its owner first tried it on in front of her looking-glass before setting out for the ball.

Look out for old paintings, tapestries and manuscripts as well while you are in the museum and make sketches of any costumes that might have a place in your project.

There are sure to be interesting churches, palaces or 'stately homes' in your district, where you could gather further evidence. Remember, though, that when people sat for their portraits they usually put on their best clothes. For everyday they wore simpler, more practical styles. So, of course, did the poorer people who could not buy or make grand dresses, or afford to have their portraits painted at all.

When we reach more recent times, say after 1850, book illustrations of the period, old copies of *Punch* or the *Illustrated London News* — which are often in libraries — will show how ordinary people really looked. Because each copy of the magazine bears an exact date you can be sure the dresses are accurate.

Fancy dress

If you are good at making clothes, even quite roughly, it would be a challenge to make a fancy dress that gives a real feeling of one particular period. Pay special attention to general outline, hair style and shoes. A wonderful effect can be achieved with very simple materials such as cast-off curtains, cardboard, crêpe paper, an old hat — and a few pins.

Spreading the fashion news

Nowadays we can learn about the latest fashions from newspapers and magazines on sale at any bookstall. It was not always so.

For centuries dressmakers in centres of fashion such as Paris would dress little dolls in the latest mode and send them about the country and abroad. How eagerly the would-be fashionable ladies must have awaited their arrival before planning new outfits!

Could you dress a small doll in a way that would give people of the past or future a correct idea of how we dress today? Have a try!

Towards the end of the eighteenth century, round about 1780, the coloured fashion print was invented. It was less trouble to make than a dressed doll and could be produced in quantity. These old fashion plates make very pretty decorations and are often displayed for sale in antique shops and second-hand book shops. See if you can track any down in your neighbourhood.

Gradual and sudden change

There are periods in which fashion develops gradually for nearly a century without a real break. Skirts grow steadily wider, waistlines rise or coats become longer, but there is no sensational change between one decade and the next.

At other times a few years will bring in a completely different outline. That happened when the pointed medieval clothes gave way to the squareness of Henry VIII's day. Some of you may have seen the television series, 'The Six Wives of Henry VIII'. Shoulders were broad, necklines were square, even shoes had squared-off toes.

From Elizabeth to the Cavaliers

Most of you will know what people looked like during the reign of Henry's daughter, Elizabeth I, from pictures of the Queen herself, of Mary Stuart, Francis Drake and Walter Raleigh. After that there was another sudden change. Round about 1620 the stiff, padded clothes in vogue since before the days of Elizabeth rapidly lost their starchiness. The upstanding collars and ruffs drooped on to the shoulders. Sleeves, skirts and breeches were no longer held out by padding but fell into loose folds. Hats became soft and wide-brimmed. Even the riding-boots sagged down. Men wore their hair long and curly, as you see in the pictures of the Cavaliers of King Charles I's reign.

An interesting collection could be made from pictures of people wearing clothes of the period between Elizabeth and Charles I

(1558–1649). Such figures often appear on postcards or in magazines and in the *TV Times* and *Radio Times*.

Stiff Elizabethan clothes, 1602 . . .

. . . give way to floppy
Charles I fashions,
1634.

Hair

By the way, what strong feelings hair styles arouse, don't they?
During the Civil War the Cavaliers mocked the shorter-haired
Puritans by calling them 'roundheads'. Hundreds of years
earlier than that churchmen were scolding the dandies of the
time in the following verse:

> Long beards heartlesse
> Painted hoods witlesse
> Gay coats gracelesse
> Make England thriftlesse.

The girls who first cut their hair short in 1917 came in for a great deal of criticism. Perhaps you can think of more recent examples . . .?

The eighteenth century

If the subject interests you, I suggest that you trace the changes of fashion between 1650 and 1700 for yourselves. That brings us to the eighteenth century which, except at the very end, was a period of gradual change.

Men wore powdered wigs and embroidered velvet coats at court. One can more or less date the portrait of an eighteenth-century man by the length of his waistcoat and the size of his wig. As the century advanced both became steadily shorter.

Fashions for women were pretty on the whole, with small waists and wide skirts, but by 1770 the court fashions had become absurdly formal and uncomfortable. Bodices were stiff, the panniered skirts could be six feet wide and towering coiffures were decorated with flowers, fruit, feathers or even model ships. In the royal courts and high society of Europe, especially in France, manners, palaces and gardens as well as clothes were very formal and artificial. To be countrified, natural or democratic was to be looked down upon.

Wigs and waistcoats (a) 1700   (b) 1735.

Towards the end of the century, however, new ideas about nature and liberty were in the air. By 1780, especially in England, which was then looked on as the home of political freedom, these ideas had begun to influence clothing. So for a few years liberty-loving people on the continent, where kings were still all-powerful, adopted English fashions to proclaim their political views.

(c) 1785.
Note that the wig
and waistcoat are
shorter than earlier
in the century.

la Candeur

A fashionable hairstyle in 1770.

The French Revolution

Then in 1789 came the French Revolution and everything was changed. In their first enthusiasm the revolutionaries wanted to start everything anew and differently. That included fashion.

By 1800 fashionable women's dresses were made of thin, usually white, material falling straight and slender from the shoulder, with a very high waistline. This line was later called the Empire style after the Emperor Napoleon I. Some girls cut their hair quite short and wore heelless slippers. One fashion expert of the time declared that a young woman's whole outfit, jewellery included, should weigh less than 4 kg (8 lb.). (What is the weight of the clothes you are wearing, shoes included, I wonder?)

Splendour in 1770.

A great influence on male clothing about that time was a certain witty dandy called Beau Brummell, who started the fashion for elegantly cut dark clothes and spotlessly clean linen. He was said to spend an hour every morning in getting his cravat exactly right. (See if you can discover more about him. You will find an entry under the name of George Brummell in the *Dictionary of National Biography* at the library.)

Crinolines and bustles

As the century advanced the Empire style lost its slender

Simplicity in 1800.

simplicity. The illustrations will show you how the female waistline dropped and tightened. Skirts grew wider and were held out by more and more petticoats till their weight became a burden.

Then in about 1850 the crinoline was invented. It was a sort of framework of hoops that allowed skirts to become even more enormous without being nearly so heavy.

The all-round fullness was gradually gathered at the back and developed into the sort of bustle dresses seen in the 1870 illustrations to *Alice through the Looking Glass.* These bustles were like short half-crinolines worn only at the back.

Beau Brummell

Skirts got fuller (1820).

Walking dresses in 1830.

Paris fashions (1840).

*The newest French
fashions (1860).*

Fashionable seaside wear (1870). The ladies in the picture are wearing bustles.

Up to the present

If the story of fashion interests you enough, you will be able to complete this short account by your own researches, and make a survey in drawings, paintings and appliqué pictures of the many changes that have occurred during the last hundred years. What do you think influences our present fashions most? Is it mass production?

An unusual aspect of fashion today is Unisex clothing. Sometimes it is quite hard in the distance to tell whether someone is a man or a woman. It will be interesting to see if the fashion lasts. Do you think the Women's Lib. movement has any connection with Unisex clothes?

One fashion sometimes brings in another. The slender Empire line of 1800 left no room for the pockets that fitted so easily into the panniered skirts of the eighteenth century, and so handbags came into vogue. If women in 1926 had not cropped their hair so short they could never have worn the 'cloche' hat. Can you think of a present-day fashion caused by mini-skirts?

6   Clothes for yourself

Examples of 'dress sense'

Knowing what suits you best

Looking smart on a small income

How about fashion and yourself? Are you always sure what will suit you?

Now that one can wear anything, from jeans to kaftans, almost anywhere we sometimes hear that the notion of being 'well dressed' or 'badly dressed' is out of date. But when you think about the people you know you will remember that some of them have a way of looking just right, whether they are wearing a patched shirt and faded jeans or are dressed up for an occasion. And it does not depend on a good-looking face or on spending a lot of money.

Dress sense

There is a mysterious quality called 'dress sense'. With some people it seems to be inborn, but it can be learnt too. Let us see if we can work out a few guide lines.

The shape and balance of clothes can matter as much as colours or fabrics. For instance, you will notice that whenever skirts with bustles or fullness at the back were in vogue hats and bonnets were worn with a forward tilt to balance the general outline. In the late Middle Ages dresses were full in front while head-dresses sloped backwards. Would you prefer a fitting or a loose bodice to go with a wide crinoline skirt?

Knowing what sort of clothes suit your type is a great help. If you have taken stock of your best and worst points, you can dress so as to emphasise the good ones and tone down the bad.

Until fairly recently men's clothes have been sombre and all of much the same pattern for more than a century. Elegance was shown by fine materials and perfect cut; bright colours were

used only for ties, blazers and pyjamas.

Now nobody is surprised to see a young man looking handsome or picturesque in clothes as exciting and colourful as those of his girl companion. And that means he must plan his clothing as carefully as she does. He can look more attractive than his father did at his age — or he can look a much worse mess!

Balance in clothes 1470 (left).

Balance in clothes 1870 (right).

Design

The answer to all these problems is DESIGN.

An exercise in design for yourself would be a 'window-shopping' expedition in which you pretend that you can choose a complete outfit, accessories included, for yourself. You could play the same game with magazine advertisements if you live in the country. It is more interesting if you have a particular sum of money in mind. As it is dream money you could fix the sum at £10, £100 or £1,000!

D

Don't choose your clothes quite separately. A girl might have a pretty hat, a smart shirt, a romantic skirt and a dashing pair of boots — and look her worst if she wore them all at the same time and they didn't go together. So try to plan your hairdo, dress and accessories as all part of the same effect and, if in doubt, choose a simple line — and, of course, the same ideas apply to young men, too.

How to look smart on a small income
There are some things you can do to appear well dressed that cost nothing at all. One of them is to stand and walk well.

Get into the habit of holding your head high, of being able to relax without slouching. When you walk, imagine that your shoulders are broad and move your legs from the hip. That makes the cheapest clothes look expensive!

You will already have noticed how much a clean, well-groomed look adds to one's general appearance.

Look at the people around you and secretly give them marks out of ten for posture, movement and grooming.

Self-consciousness is unattractive
Once you have taken trouble to plan your clothes and wear them properly, try to *forget* all about your appearance.

If you suffer from self-consciousness, you can cure it by determining not to worry about what people think of you. Turn your thoughts instead to what *you* think about *them* — or anything else that will direct your attention outwards. Not only will you look better — you will enjoy the party!

Dressmakers, shops and tailoring

7

Clothes made at home

How fashions are born

Different kinds of shops

Bespoke tailoring

Dressmaking at home

Of course the girl who can make her own clothes has a tremendous advantage. She can afford to have a great many more and they can be made to her individual taste. After learning the basic skills at home or school it is possible to take more advanced classes at a technical college or college of further education at quite a modest fee.

If we go far enough back into the past we find that practically all clothes were home-made. Even the lady of the castle did her own spinning and weaving. The invention of the sewing machine in about 1850 made an enormous difference to home dressmaking.

In the later Middle Ages cloth could be bought in the market place, and by the seventeenth century there were drapers' shops. At that time men and women would often buy a length of material to be made up by tailors or by professional dressmakers — known as seamstresses — who would come to the customer's house to fit the garments.

The court of King Louis XIV of France and his successors was a particularly luxurious and cultivated one and Paris became the chief centre of fashion in the western world.

The story of Worth

Strangely enough, it was an Englishman, Charles Frederick Worth, who created the Parisian system of *haute couture* — the higher dressmaking — in the mid-nineteenth century.

His policy was to design dresses especially to suit the looks and personality of each client and to make these dresses only from materials supplied by himself. Instead of going to his customer's house, she would have to come to his.

At first his firm ways and his ambition upset some people, but it was not long before the society ladies realised how much more elegant they would look in the sumptuous clothes he designed. When the Empress Eugénie, the wife of Napoléon III of France, became one of his clients his success was complete. The huge crinoline dresses she wore in her well-known portraits were designed by Worth, and he was the first *couturier* to display his creations on living models, then called 'mannequins'.

Centres of fashion

The Empress Eugénie with her ladies in waiting.

Paris still has a say in the world of dress, but is no longer its leader. New fashions are now born in Rome, Florence or London.

What distinguishes *haute couture* from other dress businesses is the designing skill, the extreme care and finish given to every garment, and the fact that the models are made up especially for each customer, who has to have several fittings before her dress is ready. All this makes the clothes far too expensive for the ordinary buyer.

Haute couture might well die out altogether, but each season these exclusive dress houses give shows for their rich clients and for representatives of clothes factories who are willing to pay high prices for the right to copy the new season's models. Seats at one of these dress shows for the trade can cost as much as £400. That fee includes the right to one 'toile', the calico pattern of a model.

Thus the top designers have an enormous influence on the line, colour and fabrics of the coming season. But they are not all-powerful. Their ideas must be slightly in advance of popular taste, but not out of touch with it. If they try to bring in fashions that are not in sympathy with the spirit of the time, the public will not wear them. That is what happened to the midi-skirt in 1970.

Among the 'higher dressmakers' are Dior in Paris, Hardy Amies in London and Pucci in Florence. See if you can discover some others. You may find their names in the more expensive fashion magazines such as *Vogue* and *Harper's*, which may be in the reference library.

Boutiques and perfume

Wealth is more evenly divided among people than it used to be, skilled workers earn higher wages and mass production has brought cheap but attractive clothes within the reach of the average person. These are three reasons why expensive firms find it hard to carry on when good clothes can so easily be obtained elsewhere. Those that are still in business frequently sell perfume and other luxury goods as a profitable side-line. Can you think of any perfumes sold under the name of a famous dress firm?

Other *haute-couture* firms have opened 'daughter shops' called 'boutiques' – French for a small shop – where they sell accessories and clothes. Though these are very smart and still quite expensive, they are often ready made and cheaper than the models in the 'parent' firm.

Small dress shops

There are other small dress shops, of course. Some are branches of widespread clothing businesses with their own factories. Others are run by individual owners who have invested their money in the business and take the greatest interest in decorating their sales rooms and selecting clothes to please both themselves and the buying public. In the trade these small businesses are known by the quaint name of 'Madam shops'.

If you live in a town where there are several dress shops, you could go on an expedition with friends and decide which shop shows the most attractive clothes and the best display arrangement. Distinguish, if you can, between branches of big firms and individually-owned shops. If the town is big enough there are sure to be big stores with several departments too.

Department stores and chain stores

One advantage of big stores is that you can wander through them, deciding at your leisure whether or what to buy. A department store generally sells a variety of goods, but clothes are the most important and are sold in different divisions labelled 'Model gowns', 'Inexpensive dresses', 'Knitwear', 'Men's wear', and so on. Some of these stores have branches in a number of towns.

A chain store usually consists of one great hall where the goods are divided among counters rather than departments and the prices tend to be lower and more on the same level.

If possible, inspect both kinds of large store and see if you notice any other differences between them.

Supposing you were to become a sales assistant, which of all the above kinds of shop would you prefer to work in?

Mail order

Another way of buying clothes is by mail order, cutting out shops altogether. I expect you have often seen mail order advertise-

ments in the newspapers. Although there is some risk of disappointment when one buys goods unseen, the garments are often very satisfactory and many people enjoy shopping this way because they like getting parcels.

A famous chain store.

Clothes shops for men

Men's clothes can be bought in more or less the same kinds of shop as women's.

Ready-made suits used not to be of top quality, but nowadays they are often made of the best materials, are well cut and can be slightly altered to fit the wearer exactly. Some of them cost a lot of money too!

Bespoke tailoring

It is still more expensive, however, for a man to have his clothes made especially for him by a tailor. This is known as bespoke tailoring. The best-known bespoke tailors in the world are in Savile Row and neighbouring parts of London's

West End. Here, for not less than £100, you will get an expertly-cut suit of the finest material.

Tailoring is a highly skilled craft, and the suit will have to be fitted on the customer several times before it is passed as fit to wear. After that it should last for years and never lose that well-cut look. Rich men come from all over the world to buy their suits from London tailors.

Different ways of dressing

A strange situation exists at present in the world of men's clothes. There are at least three quite different styles of dressing, each with its own sort of shop and each suggesting a different set of ideas about life.

If a city clerk turned up at work dressed as a hippy or a Hell's Angel, he would certainly be sent home to change. On the other hand, would the same clerk, wearing his collar and tie and neat dark suit, get a warm welcome from the hippy or skinhead groups?

By the way, all businesses that sell direct to the public are called 'retail outlets'.

Mass production

8

Clothes made in factories

Designing, planning, cutting, sewing and selling

Making garments by hand in the nineteenth century

Factories that make clothes

But where do the goods in the retail shops come from?

Some of the biggest clothes shops, especially the great chain stores, have their own design teams and order garments to to be specially made for them in the factories.

More often factories have their own designers working in consultation with the management. After much thought as to which styles will prove most saleable, hundreds or thousands of identical garments are shaped to the same pattern, but made up in different sizes and perhaps in different colours.

When a garment is manufactured by the thousand, every inch of material saved means a thousand inches saved per batch, just as every minute of machine time saved adds up to many valuable hours.

Therefore the saving of time, labour and material achieved by these methods keeps down the price of the finished product.

That is the purpose of mass production.

Visiting a factory

It is fascinating to see in action the process of manufacturing clothes.

Many of the larger garment-making firms will show parties over their factories. If you are interested, why not see if your teacher can arrange a visit for you?

Every firm has its own methods, but roughly speaking the process of manufacture goes more or less like this:

The design section

The designer works out an idea for a dress and makes sketches of it, pinning pieces of the suggested fabric to the paper.

The garment must not only be smart and attractive. It must also make a profit for the firm. Therefore the price of the material, the cost of manufacture and the taste of the buying public are all matters the designer has to consider. After the first sketches are completed there has to be a good deal of discussion with other heads of departments.

Choosing the fabric

Another important job is that of fabric-buying. Thousands of yards of material will be bought at a time, so it has to be cleverly chosen and carefully tested.

Sometimes the textile inspires the designer with ideas as to how it can best be used, at other times it may be ordered specially to carry out a design.

The first sample

A 'toile' is now made. That expression was used in the last chapter and is the French word for linen cloth, pronounced 'twahl'. It is the first version of the designed garment, made by pinning and draping cheap calico on a life-size stand.

The next step is for the designer's cutter to make a pattern of the garment, from which a sample is made in the actual material to be used. When this sample has been inspected and approved by the various heads of departments concerned, and perhaps altered a little, a new pattern is cut. In order to save a centimetre ($\frac{1}{2}$ in.) here and half a centimetre ($\frac{1}{4}$ in.) there, a so-called 'marker' fits the different parts of it — collar, sleeves, bodice, etc. — together so cleverly that the whole thing looks like a jigsaw puzzle. Once cut out, the cardboard shapes are ready to go down to the 'production floor'.

The production department

Downstairs is the huge machine room where a hundred or so men and women are working at many different jobs.

The machine room in a clothing factory. This shows the fabric cutting table.

Layer on layer of fabric is stretched out on long tables by machine. Swift, dangerous 'band knives' cut through a hundred thicknesses of cloth as if it were butter. Do not speak to the cutter while he is using this mechanical knife for, if his attention is distracted for even a moment, he may cut off his finger. A great many women and girls are seated at machines for joining, buttonholing, trimming and so on, each doing a different part of the dress. Some of these machines are capable of sewing 9,000 stitches an hour.

The machinists work hard because they are paid 'piecework' rates, that is, by the amount of work they complete. There are a number of supervisors to see that everything goes smoothly, and the work is inspected over and over again as it progresses.

How the goods get into the shops

Clothes manufacturers used to sell their products to wholesalers who in turn sold them to retail shops at a profit. That system appears to be on the way out.

Big factories often run their own show rooms in the more fashionable parts of the town. There, models display samples of

Clothing machinists at work.

next season's styles to buyers from shops or to agents. Thus many of the finished goods will have been ordered months before they are made.

A number of the larger clothes-manufacturing firms, however, have their own shops. Sometimes they have 'shops within shops'. Those are departments within a big store that specialise in clothes made by one particular manufacturing firm. Have you noticed any of them in your town?

Outside work

The chief clothing manufacturers do not have all the garments made in the factory. They send out a great deal of work to outside workers. Patterns and materials go to be made up by small firms owning a workshop with a few machines, or even to an individual working at home.

Costs and prices

If you like numbers, it may amuse you to work out the following
simple puzzle.

To make one dress it costs the manufacturer £3 for material,
£2 for wages and £1 for overheads and other expenses. The
firm's own retail shop sells the dress at a profit of $33\frac{1}{3}$ per cent
$(=\frac{1}{3})$. What price does the customer have to pay?

I have called this a puzzle but, in fact, it is the sort of calculation
people in the clothes trade have to be making every day.

9 Careers and training

Opportunities in fashion

Buying fabric, making patterns

Mary Quant and other designers

Tailoring and fashion modelling

Amazingly, the clothing industry is the fifth largest in the United Kingdom. How many people does it employ would you guess? Roughly 10,000 − 100,000 − 500,000 or one million? Look for the answer at the end of this chapter.

This great industry offers countless opportunities for different sorts of careers.

Designing: the dream and the reality

The fashion career that people usually think of first is that of designer. We imagine ourselves dreaming up exciting dresses and either making drawings of them or draping materials on a dummy figure till we get the right effect. It is true that these activities are part of the work. But, as we saw in the last chapter, there is much more to it than that.

The designer has to have a feeling for line, colour, form and texture. He or she also needs to know about cut, textiles, costs, what sort of clothes the firm's customers will want to buy and what machinery there is in the factory making the clothes. For instance, before deciding on a style that includes a great many buttonholes and pintucks the designer must make sure that there are buttonholing and pintucking machines available. Otherwise there will be what is called a 'bottleneck', and production will be badly held up at that point.

So, although it has been said that a designer is 'born not made', it is important to have a proper training. But what sort of training? There are different views on that subject.

Art school training

The very ambitious might begin with an art course. A number of art schools in the United Kingdom, such as St Martin's School of Art, London or the Leicester School of Art, run 3-year diploma courses in dress design.

The first year is spent on general art training and the next two on clothes design, including the practical and technical sides. To enter these courses the student has to be 18 years of age and have five O-levels.

Stage design

An art school training is a necessity for a designer of theatrical costumes, but that is an altogether different profession. One can be a good modern dress designer without being a good stage designer, and the opposite is just as true.

To design clothes for the theatre one needs a good knowledge of the theatre, art and history. It is more important for stage costumes to be right for the play and the character than to suit the looks of the wearer. The stage picture as a whole is more important than any one costume.

College of Fashion and other courses

Quite apart from colleges of art there are several colleges specialising in the art and methods of clothes-making. For example, there is the College of Fashion and Clothing Technology in London (see useful addresses and books on page 68). It is an impressive building with a fine library, lecture halls and long corridors lined with students' paintings.

Here the would-be designer can take a 3-year diploma course which teaches not only the principles of fashion and design but also about clothes manufacture, textiles, dressmaking, pattern-cutting and business management. This course can be started at the age of 16 if you have three O-levels or a good CSE. Among the other subjects taught there are tailoring, millinery, embroidery and clothing-machine engineering.

Some of these are 3-year diploma courses, others are 2-year courses leading to the City and Guilds examinations. Several subjects can be studied in part-time or evening classes.

There are colleges of this kind in London, Manchester, Belfast, Leeds, Teesside and other places.

Although a designer must have ideas of her – or his – own, it is vital to keep up with all that is newest on the fashion front. So he or she must go to dress shows, particularly the ready-to-wear shows in Paris and Italy, and even look around the London shops. New ideas can crop up in all sorts of unexpected ways. In large firms there is a whole team of designers, in small firms the designer sometimes has to do the pattern-cutting and grading as well.

The remarks in chapter 6 on planning your own clothes apply to commercial design as well.

A good exercise for a future designer is to plan a dress or a whole outfit as if it were really to be manufactured. Think out and draw your design, find the right materials, estimate the quantity needed – with the width and pattern of the material in mind – and work out how much it would cost. Do not forget items such as zip-fasteners and thread. You will have to notice the drape of the fabric and whether the pattern – if any – has to be arranged all in the same direction.

Other interesting careers in fashion

Designing is far from being the only interesting work in the world of clothes.

(a) The person who buys textile fabric for a firm has to be artistic, fashion-conscious, practical and, above all, to be very know-ledgeable about cloth. The job may involve a good deal of travel in search of the right materials. Years of experience go to make a good buyer.

(b) Another very skilled occupation is pattern-cutting. This is often a man's job. It has been described as 'engineering in cloth'. A pattern-cutter has to be able to imagine how flat shapes will look in the round and how curved shapes will look when laid flat – as well as how to get the most out of a length of fabric.

(c) The work of grading a pattern into different sizes also requires skill. There are considerably more openings for pattern-cutters and graders than there are for designers. Some firms deal in paper patterns only.

All these crafts can be studied at various polytechnics and colleges of further education. The county education officer's department would be able to give you information about such courses. And if you are interested in that sort of training it is worth finding out about scholarships and grants. But here comes a word of warning.

Caution!

Managers of clothing factories say that 'paper qualifications', as they call diplomas and certificates, are all very well, but that they are almost useless without practical work in a real factory. Factory managers feel annoyed when people who have just left college expect to go to the top right away.

If a new employee has good paper qualifications the best way to succeed is to be prepared to take quite a humble job for a few months in order to gain experience. Perhaps it is best of all to do some ordinary, practical work in a clothing factory before going to college at all.

A new sort of clothing business

A new type of clothing firm has arisen of recent years, neither *haute couture,* department store nor boutique. It is a firm headed by a designer and aimed principally at the production of reasonably priced but highly fashionable clothes for youngish people. It has its own workrooms, but instead of running a factory it sends samples of the garments designed to be made up in quantity by big manufacturers.

An example

Perhaps the pioneer in this field was the firm of Mary Quant, so I will take that as an example.

Mary Quant herself always wanted to be a dress designer. Her father and mother were teachers and her grandfather had been a Welsh miner. They knew what it was to have anxieties about money, so they allowed their daughter to go to an art school, but only on condition that she studied for an art teacher's certificate. Her very first job after leaving the school was in a hat shop where

E

she designed expensive hats all day for a salary of £2·50 a week! While they were both art students a young man called Alexander Plunkett-Greene formed a great admiration for the shy and talented girl. He suggested that they should start a small dress business together. They did more than that. They got married.

Their idea was to produce smart young clothes that need not last for years, to be sold at prices most people could afford. They worked very hard but did not make much money at first because they knew so little about the business side. Then they joined up with a third partner, a fashion photographer who understood how to raise capital and run a business. They thought his plan of attaching a coffee bar to their first dress shop, 'Bazaar', was a crazy idea, but to their surprise it was as successful as the dresses and helped the business a lot.

After that they never looked back, although the hard work continued as before. Other branches of Bazaar were opened; the coffee bar went, but was replaced by a restaurant. After a while the retail shops were closed. Mary Quant Ltd began to produce a wider range of goods: knitwear, shoes, cosmetics, even bed-linen. The designs were made up into samples in their own work-rooms, then sent to be mass-produced in outside factories, and sold to shops and stores in many countries.

The birth of the mini-skirt

At first some of the factory managers thought the Quant clothes were too 'way out'. It was better to deal with more open-minded firms. One day Mary saw a sweater in a factory. 'Make me one like that', she said, 'but six inches longer.'

The manufacturer thought it a strange idea but carried it out. It was sold not as a sweater but as a dress much shorter than had been fashionable till then — and so the mini-dress was born!

And since mini-skirts needed to be worn with tights, Mary Quant Ltd branched out into tights and later on into all sorts of other products.

It seemed as if everything they touched turned to gold. But, in fact, the very speed of their success might have ruined them. For seven years they were never quite without money worries, because while the orders poured in, they needed money to

Mary Quant.

pay the factories for making the goods ordered, and banks were not always keen to lend it.

All ended happily, however. Today Quant clothes and products are sold all over the world. The 'turnover' of the cosmetic branch alone is £5 million a year!

A Mary Quant design.

Other designer firms

There are now a number of similar firms, though each has its distinct character. Among them are: Jean Muir, Ossie Clark, Geoff Banks. Have you heard of others?

The production floor

But what about the people making the clothes in mass-production factories?

Many of the ordinary machinists are content to stay as they are. They can make quite good money once they are used to the work. Others are more ambitious.

Opportunities if you want them enough

A firm is only too glad to find a keen, intelligent worker. Promising workers, men or women, on the production floor can rise to be supervisors or even managers, but not until they have proved themselves.

Management

The clothing industry has now become such big business that there are more and more opportunities on the managerial side, especially for men. They include planning, accountancy and public relations. There is also a growing demand for clothing engineering and for market and textile research. The Clothing Institute can advise on training for these careers (see useful addresses and books on page 68).

Tailoring

Mass-production tailoring is run on much the same lines as other kinds of large-scale clothes manufacture, and there are many courses on the subject at the various colleges.

With bespoke tailoring things are rather different. Here the old tradition of apprenticeship lingers on.

If his parents agree, an apprentice undertakes to work for his employer for five years. In return the master tailor promises to teach him the whole craft of tailoring and not to ask for overtime work during the first three years.

There is usually a 6-month or 1-year trial period on each side. Occasionally the apprentice may be sent to outside courses at a technical college. A learner is not bound by the same contract.

Fashion modelling

Girls who are lucky enough to have pretty faces and slender figures are often told by their friends that they ought to become fashion models. It certainly sounds a glamorous career. If you are highly successful it *is* glamorous — at times and for a while.

There is a demand for attractive girls to show off the clothes at dress shows and in shops, factory show rooms and photographs. It is not as easy as it looks, of course. Nothing is.

It is almost essential to have some training, which can be taken at a number of colleges of fashion or private modelling schools. There the instructors will start by criticising your hair-do, your figure, the way you walk and the way you wear your clothes. By the time you leave you will have learnt how to make the best of yourself, how to sit gracefully, move beautifully, show off clothes, and smile whether you feel like it or not. Those are qualities it is pleasant to have even if you never become a model.

The snag is that the job does not lead on to anything higher and, as the years go by, you tend to get less work rather than more.

There are other careers connected with fashion — fashion journalists and photographers . . .. Can you think of some more? If you were to work in the clothing industry, what line would you choose?

By the way, the answer to the question at the beginning of this chapter is 500,000 (half a million).

*A Mary Quant fashion
photograph.*

10 Salesmanship, imports, exports and jobs

Retail selling

Sales assistants

Clothes from abroad

Looking for your first job

A side of the fashion trade we have not yet mentioned is retail selling.

Almost the same might be said of salesmen and women as of designers: 'They are born not made.' Don't consider becoming a sales assistant unless *you like people*. Next time you are in a clothes shop notice how the assistants behave and privately award them marks for it.

A few of them treat you as if you were just a nuisance. They could not be less interested in you or the stock. Their chief thought is 'When will it be closing time?' and oh! how the hours drag for them!

An opposite fault is sometimes seen in shops that pay a commission on sales (possibly $2\frac{1}{2}$ per cent of the retail value of everything sold). A too-eager sales assistant pounces on you before you have time to look around and presses you to buy something you do not really want.

Neither of those types will get high marks because the customer is unlikely to come back for more.

The perfect sales assistant never tries to hurry you or force you to buy, yet appears really interested in your wants and knows all about the stock, that is to say the goods in the department. Even if you buy nothing the first time you will not be afraid to come again.

What is more, being interested in the customer and the job really does make the time pass quickly!

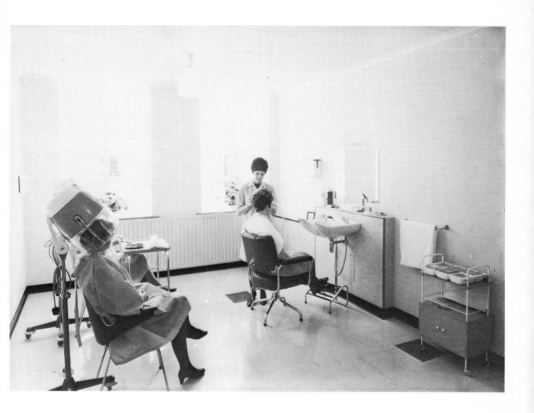

Sales jobs

There are selling jobs to be had in small shops, boutiques and big department stores. The last often have their own canteens and social clubs. After some years a keen sales assistant can be made a departmental buyer or get some other interesting post with a good salary.

Our best-known chain store dealing in clothes gives its staff special privileges – free dental and medical advice, free chiropody and very cheap hairdressing in the firm's time, Christmas bonuses and very generous wedding presents.

When I asked the staff manageress what she looked for in applicants for sales jobs she replied, 'a pleasant manner, a neat appearance and alertness'. With these gifts and a few years of experience it is possible to be promoted to supervisor or even higher well-paid positions.

Young men who go into firms of this kind with at least two 'A' levels become 'management trainees' and have good chances of

A Marks and Spencer staff hairdressing salon. Lunch can be served under a hairdryer.

promotion if they show the right qualities.

If requested, such firms will often arrange for parties to inspect the store and see the way it works.

Import and export

Not all the buying and selling goes on in our own country. Many of the clothes sold in our shops were made abroad and have been imported. On the other hand Great Britain sells, that is to say exports, a great deal of her clothing production to other countries.

In 1971 the United Kingdom exported nearly £130 million worth of clothing. But we *imported* clothing to the value of £178 million – an average of more than £3 worth to each man, woman and child in the country.

Look at the labels inside your clothes, or in garments for sale in shops, and see how many names of different producing countries you can find. You could add them to your picture map if you are making one. The words 'Empire Made' usually mean Hong Kong.

The College of Fashion and Clothing Technology (see page 55) gives a special course on export. Knowing one or two foreign languages is particularly useful in this branch of the trade.

The Rag Trade

Did you know that the clothing industry is sometimes nicknamed the 'Rag Trade'?

Some people call it a rat race too, meaning that it is a ruthless struggle to get on, without regard for other people. Like so many sayings, there is some truth in it but not the whole truth.

One certainly needs determination to reach the top – or anywhere near it. A young designer who was top of her year in the Fashion and Clothing Design examination at her college told me that it took her six months to land her first job! After that there was no further difficulty in finding work. What one needs in the fashion world, she says, is confidence, determination – and of course skill. Now she has made the grade she finds it an interesting, exciting, career.

Looking for a job

Supposing you are trained and qualified as a designer, pattern-cutter or for some other work in the fashion trade, what should your next step be?

You have to overcome that well-known stumbling block in the path of every beginner: 'We cannot give you a job if you have not had any practical experience!' So how can you get that first experience?

Some are lucky enough to have useful introductions, a few find jobs through their colleges. Positions are advertised in trade papers such as the *Draper's Record.* There are also employment agencies for the clothing trade. One of the best known is the Star Agency. It may be necessary to accept a fairly modest job at first but, if you are good at your work, persistence will win through in the end!

Useful addresses and books

Addresses
The Clothing Institute, 17 Henrietta Street, London WC2 will give advice about training and qualifications as well as the addresses of clothing factories in your district that can be viewed by school parties. The College of Fashion and Clothing Technology is at 20 John Prince's Street, London W1 and has a branch at 100 Curtain Road, London EC2.

Other fashion colleges are in Manchester, Leeds and Belfast.

The county education officer is always willing to give information and advice on training.

Books
What we all wear: the Raw Materials of clothing by Owen Webster (Harrap, 1968)

From Fibres to Fabrics by Elizabeth Gale (Allman, 1968)

Textiles: Fiber to Fabric by M. D. Potter and B. P. Corbman (McGraw, 1959)

A Fashion Alphabet by Janey Ironside (Michael Joseph, 1968)

World Costumes by Angela Bradshaw (A. & C. Black, 1952)

Folk and Festival Costume of the World by R. Turner Wilcox (Batsford, 1966)

Costume through the Ages by James Laver (Thames & Hudson, 1963)

Dress by James Laver (Murray, 1966)

Taste and Fashion by James Laver (Harrap, 1945)

Costume in Greek Classic Drama by Iris Brooke (Methuen, 1962)

English Costume by Iris Brooke (A. & C. Black, 7 vols)

A History of English Costume by Iris Brooke (Methuen, 1968)

Mediaeval Theatre Costume by Iris Brooke (A. & C. Black, 1967)

Outline of English Costume by D. Yarwood (Batsford, 1967)

Everyday Costume in Britain by Audrey Barfoot (Batsford, 1961)

Look at Clothes by Pearl Binder (Hamish Hamilton, 1959)

Corsets and Crinolines by Norah Waugh (Batsford, 1954)
Cut of Men's Clothes. 1600–1900 by Norah Waugh (Faber & Faber, 1964)
Occupational Costume by P. Cunnington and C. Lucas (A. & C. Black, 1967)
Introducing Pattern Cutting, Grading` and Modelling by Margaritha Goulbourn (Batsford, 1971)
Fashion Design by Joanne Brogden (Studio Vista, 1971)

Acknowledgments

The author and publishers would like to thank those listed below for help and for permission to reproduce illustrations: The Clothing Institute, The College of Fashion and Technology, Marks & Spencer Ltd, Mary Quant Ltd, Messrs Ellis & Goldstein, Musée National du Château de Compiègne, National Portrait Gallery, Trustees of the British Museum (Natural History), Victoria and Albert Museum, Vogue Magazine.

The local search series

Editor : Mrs Molly Harrison MBE, FRSA

This book is one of a highly successful series designed to help young people to look inquiringly and critically at particular aspects of the world about them. It encourages them to think for themselves, to seek first-hand information from other people, to make the most of visits to interesting places, and to record their discoveries and their experiences.

Many boys and girls enjoy detective work of this kind and find it fun to look for evidence and to illustrate their findings in ways that appeal to them. Such lively activities are equally rewarding whether carried out individually or in a group.

Already published

The English Village
Dennis R. Mills

The English Home
Molly Harrison

The Public Library
Frank Atkinson

Living Creatures of an English Home
Olive Royston

The Public Park
Herbert L. Edlin

Farms and Farming
Rowland W. Purton

The Post Office
Olive Royston

Looking at the Countryside
Annesley Voysey

A Home of Your Own
Margaret Kirby

The Theatre
Olive Ordish

Graves and Graveyards
Kenneth Lindley

Rivers and Canals
Rowland W. Purton

Museums and Galleries
Molly Harrison

Markets and Fairs
Rowland W. Purton

Trees and Timbers
Herbert L. Edlin

Dress and Fashion
Olive Ordish

Looking at Language
J. A. Robinson

Forthcoming

Factories, Forges and Foundries
Roy Christian

The Town Hall
Olive Royston

Seaside and Seacoast
Kenneth Lindley